$\mathcal{D}$
IS FOR DEMOCRACY

by KRISTIN CASHORE

Editorial Offices: Glenview, Illinois • Parsippany, New Jersey • New York, New York

Sales Offices: Needham, Massachusetts • Duluth, Georgia • Glenview, Illinois
Coppell, Texas • Sacramento, California • Mesa, Arizona

Leaders such as George Washington, Benjamin Franklin, and James Madison took part in the Constitutional Convention.

The Constitution is Born

In 1787 the United States of America was a very young country. The country's leaders agreed that the country needed to be strong, but many of them disagreed about how to best accomplish this.

In May of 1787, important leaders from all over the nation met in Philadelphia, Pennsylvania. This meeting is called the Constitutional Convention. The leaders talked, listened, and argued. Over several months, they created the Constitution of the United States of America.

This Constitution created a very special **government** for the United States. It explained how the nation should be run. Today our country's government is still based on the Constitution. Let's take a look at the document that has made our country strong and free.

The first few lines of the Constitution explain why it is being written. It says the Constitution will make a government that is strong and just. It will keep the country peaceful, and it will keep the country's **citizens** safe. It will promise liberty to all citizens, both in 1787 and in the future.

Next, the Constitution explains the kind of government the nation will have. This government has three very important branches, or parts. Read on to learn about the three branches of government.

This is the Constitution of the United States of America.

The House of Representatives and the Senate are in separate parts of the Capitol building. The House and the Senate debate and vote separately. The chamber of the House of Representatives is pictured here.

The Legislative Branch

One branch of government, the **legislative branch**, is called Congress. Congress legislates, or makes new laws. Congress has two parts. One part is the House of Representatives, and the other part is the Senate.

Each state is represented by two senators. The number of representatives that each state has, however, depends on the population of the state. For example, California has more people than Alaska has. Therefore, California has more representatives in Congress than Alaska has.

How does Congress make new laws?

A law starts out as a **bill**, which is an idea for a law. Members of Congress debate whether the bill should be passed or not before they vote. If the bill passes in both the House and the Senate, then it is sent to the President. If the President thinks the bill should be passed too, it is signed. It then becomes a law. However, if the President does not like the bill, it is vetoed, or rejected, and sent back to Congress. Congress can vote on the bill again. If two-thirds of both the House and the Senate vote for the bill, then it will become a law, even if the President does not agree with it.

The legislative branch has other jobs as well. It raises money for the government and creates new courts.

Both the House of Representatives and the Senate meet inside this building, which is called the Capitol.

The Executive Branch

The **executive branch** includes the President and the Vice President. It also includes the people who help the President. The executive branch enforces the laws.

The President is the most powerful person in the executive branch, and in the whole government. Therefore, there are many rules about the presidency. For example, the President must be at least thirty-five years old and must have been born in the United States. Also, the President may only be elected into office twice. Each term of office lasts four years. This rule is different

for members of Congress. The terms of senators are six years, and they can be elected over and over. The terms of representatives last two years, and they can also be elected over and over.

The Constitution gives the President a lot of power. The President can sign or veto laws. The President is the commander of the armed forces. The President can make treaties, or formal agreements, with other countries. The President can choose judges and other important people in the government.

The President of the United States lives and works in the White House.

The Judicial Branch

The **judicial branch** is made up of the Supreme Court, the highest court in the United States, and other federal courts.

The judges of the Supreme Court and other federal courts are chosen by the President. Before a judge can join the court, however, the Senate must agree with the President's choice.

The judges who sit on the Supreme Court are called justices. Supreme Court justices can stay on the court for the rest of their lives. This is true for all federal judges.

Above the columns of the Supreme Court building are the words, "Equal Justice Under Law."

Today there are nine justices on the Supreme Court. The decisions of the Court are final.

The Constitution gives the Supreme Court the power to interpret laws. This means that the Court decides if a law is unfair or if a person has been treated unfairly. The Supreme Court can overturn a law. Because it is the highest court in the nation, the Supreme Court's decision is always final. The Supreme Court is located in Washington, D.C. The other federal courts are found in every region of the country.

Checks and Balances

The writers of the Constitution did not want any branch of the government to become too powerful. They made sure that this did not happen by using a system of checks and balances.

The three branches of government balance each other out. Each branch checks, or limits, the power of the other branches. For example, the President may veto a bill that Congress has passed. However, Congress may pass a law that the President has vetoed. The Supreme Court may overturn a law that Congress has passed.

Here is another example. The President chooses justices and other officials in the government. However, the President cannot just choose anyone. If the Senate does not agree with the President's choice, then the President must choose again.

The people's right to vote also protects the way our nation is run. The United States is a **democracy**. Citizens decide who will hold positions of leadership. If a leader uses power poorly or in an unfair way, then the citizens can decide not to elect that leader again.

The checks and balances in the Constitution help to keep the government fair.

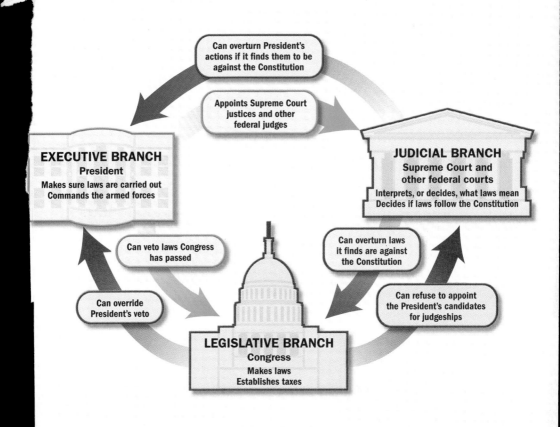

Can overturn President's actions if it finds them to be against the Constitution

Appoints Supreme Court justices and other federal judges

EXECUTIVE BRANCH
President
Makes sure laws are carried out
Commands the armed forces

JUDICIAL BRANCH
Supreme Court and other federal courts
Interprets, or decides, what laws mean
Decides if laws follow the Constitution

Can veto laws Congress has passed

Can overturn laws it finds are against the Constitution

Can override President's veto

Can refuse to appoint the President's candidates for judgeships

LEGISLATIVE BRANCH
Congress
Makes laws
Establishes taxes

The Constitution created a system of checks and balances.

The Bill of Rights names some of the most important American freedoms.

The Bill of Rights and Other Amendments

The writers of the Constitution took one more step to make sure the government would be fair. They made it possible to add to the Constitution, or even change it, if necessary. An addition to the Constitution is called an **amendment**.

The first ten amendments to the Constitution are called the Bill of Rights. They are a list of basic rights that are promised to all citizens. These rights include freedom of speech, freedom to meet in groups, freedom of the press, and freedom of religion. They include the right of a crime suspect to be treated fairly. They say that punishments for crimes should not be cruel.

The United States is known for being the land of the free. For many people, the Bill of Rights describes American freedom best.

The first ten amendments are not the only important amendments in the Constitution. The 13th Amendment ended slavery. The 15th Amendment gave men of all races the right to vote. The 19th Amendment gave women the right to vote. The 26th Amendment lowered the voting age to eighteen.

The writers of the Constitution believed amendments should be made to the Constitution. Amendments allow the Constitution to change as the world does.

The Bill of Rights gives people the right to form groups and protest. People protest for things like civil rights, women's rights, and peace.

Building a Strong Democracy

When the writers of the Constitution got together in 1787, they knew that the national government needed to be stronger. However, they also wanted the nation to be a land of freedom. To do this, they built a strong government with checks and balances. They wrote a strong Constitution that could be amended, if necessary. They also made sure that the United States would be a democracy, where every citizen could take part in the government.

The people who created the Constitution hoped it would be the foundation for a strong government.

The bald eagle is our national bird. It is a symbol of strength and freedom. It represents all that our founding leaders hoped for.

The Constitution has given us a solid foundation for our government. The people elect most of the nation's leaders. The legislative, executive, and judicial branches work well together. The best thing about the Constitution is that it is a living document. It grows and changes as our country grows and changes.

The writers of the Constitution hoped that their plan of government would work both in 1787 and in the future. Today the Constitution is still seen as an important document. The United States is a healthy democracy, and we owe the founding leaders of 1787 our thanks for their contribution.

Glossary

amendment an addition

bill an idea for a law that is put into writing

citizen an official member of a country

democracy a system of government in which every citizen has the right to take part

executive branch the part of the government that makes sure our nation's laws are followed

government the leaders who run a country and the laws that the citizens of the country follow

judicial branch the part of the government that decides if our nation's laws are fair under the Constitution

legislative branch the part of the government that makes our nation's laws